ALEXANDRIA CITY DIRECTORY

1791

Marjorie D. Tallichet
Alexandria Library
Lloyd House

HERITAGE BOOKS
2013

HERITAGE BOOKS

AN IMPRINT OF HERITAGE BOOKS, INC.

Books, CDs, and more—Worldwide

For our listing of thousands of titles see our website
at
www.HeritageBooks.com

Published 2013 by
HERITAGE BOOKS, INC.
Publishing Division
5810 Ruatan Street
Berwyn Heights, Md. 20740

Heritage Books by the author:
Alexandria City Directory, 1791
Alexandria, Virginia, City and County 1850 Census

International Standard Book Numbers
Paperbound: 978-1-55613-003-8
Clothbound: 978-0-7884-6877-3

INTRODUCTION AND GENERAL INDEX

The Alexandria Library presents to its patrons a city directory for the year 1791 which is based on a record made by George Deneale and presented to Dennis Ramsay on 28 February 1791 of the tax returns on houses and lots in the city of Alexandria.

The Directory is divided into three parts. The first is an alphabetic arrangement of all the names listed in the record with the information concerning the street location of the property and the ownership of the property placed next to the name.

The second part is a listing of the residents by street. Refer to the first part to determine whether the resident was an owner or an occupier.

The third part is a listing by occupation. This information was pulled from census reports of 1794-1797.

We trust that the Directory will be an asset to those interested in Alexandria and its development.

M.D. Tallichet, Ed.

Alexandria
           Error Excepted
                       Dennis Ramsay Commissioner

Alexandria
   I do hereby certifie that the foregoing list   on
return of tax on houses and lotts in the town of
Alexandria is a true copy ex´d by the vouchers set´d
by the Com: this 28 February 17 91.

                       Test. G. Deneale

ADAM
Robert, (estate), owner;
Adam Bloss, occupier,
Fairfax St.; Adam
Bloss, occupier,
Queen St.; Thos.
Crandell, occupier,
on the wharf; Thos.
Hannah, occupier,
Queen St.; William
Hodgson, occupier, on
the wharf; Suky King,
occupier, Fairfax
St.; Harry Lattimore,
occupier, near Prin-
cess St.; Mrs. Tal-
bot, occupier, Queen
St.; Thos. White,
occupier, Fairfax St.

ALLISON
Elizabeth, occupier;
William Bushby, own-
er, near Fairfax St.
John, occupier, seaman;
Charles Bryan, owner,
King St.
Patrick, owner; Henry
Hiker, occupier, King
St.; no one listed as
occupier, Cameron St.
Robert, owner; Buchan &
Patton, occupier,
King St.

ANDERSON
Eliz., occupier; William
Anderson, decd., own-
er, King St.
Eliz., (decd., heirs of),
owner, King St.

ANDERSON & JAMIESON
occupier; Robert Lyle
(estate), owner,
Royal St.

ARELL
David, owner & occupier,
Wilkes St.
Richard, owner & occu-
pier, Duke St.; John
Duffy, occupier,
Royal St.; William
Farrel, occupier,
Fairfax St.; Wm.
McBride, occupier,
Fairfax St.; Henry
McCue, occupier,
Royal St.; William
Marks, occupier,
Fairfax St.; Peter
Pile, occupier, Royal
St.; Jonah Thompson,
occupier, King St.
Samuel, owner; Hannah
Chamberlin, occupier,
Duke St.; James Chat-
ham, occupier, Duke
St.

ASHTON
Rich. W., owner; Edw. K.
Thompson, occupier,
Water St.

BAKER
William, owner; John Haw-
kins, occupier, Fair-
fax St.

3

BALFOUR
James, occupier, brewer;
    Betty Steuart, owner,
    King St.

BEALE
John, occupier; John
    Muir, owner, King St.

BEATIS
John, occupier; Richard
    Ratcliff, owner, St.
    Asaph

BELL
Charles, occupier;
    William Hunter Jr.,
    owner, Queen St.

BENCE
Adam, owner & occupier,
    near Gibbon St.

BIRD
William, owner, cooper,
    Lanty Crowe, Fairfax
    St.; John Kean,
    occupier, Fairfax St.

BLOSS
Adam, occupier; Robert
    Adam (estate), owner,
    Fairfax St.; occu-
    pier, Robert Adam
    (estate), owner,
    Queen St.

BLUNT
Washer, occupier, block-
    maker; William Her-
    bert, owner, Water
    St.; owner & occu-
    pier, near Prince St.

BOND
Richard, owner; Ann
    Molds, occupier,
    Fairfax St.

BORER
John, owner; Samuel
    Goods, occupier,
    Water St.

BOYER
John, owner, cooper;
    Thomas Crandel, occu-
    pier, Union St.

BOZWELL
occupier; Josiah Watson,
    owner, Fairfax St.

BRIGHT
John, owner & occupier,
    Fairfax St.

BROCKET
Robert, owner & occupier,
    Washington St.

BROMLEY
William, owner & occu-
    pier, near Fairfax
    St.

BROWN
William, owner & occu-
    pier, Fairfax St.
occupier; Thomas Kirkpat-
    rick (estate), owner,
    Water St.

BRYAN
Charles, owner; John
    Allison, occupier,
    King St.

4

BRYCE
Hannah, owner; Andrew
Knower, occupier
Prince St.
William, occupier;
William Hunter, Sr.,
owner, Union St.

BUCHAN & PATTON
occupier; Robert Allison,
owner, King St.

BUDD
Henry, occupier; William
Hunter, Jr. owner,
Prince St.

BURNETT
Mary, owner; Mrs.
Chevalier, occupier,
Love Alley

BURNS
John, owner & occupier,
Fairfax St.
Patrick, occupier;
Michael Madden,
owner, Prince St.

BUSHBY
Joseph, occupier; William
Bushby, owner, Fair-
fax St.
William, owner, painter;
Elizabeth Allison,
occupier, near Fair-
fax St.; Joseph Bush-
by, occupier, Fairfax
St.; Langston, occu-
pier, near Duke St.;
Thomas McKnab, occu-
pier, Fairfax St.;
Ann Newman, occupier,

BUSHBY (continued)
Fairfax St.; Polly,
occupier, near Fair-
fax St.; Adam Steer,
occupier, Fairfax
St.; no one named as
occupier, near Fair-
fax St.

BUTCHER
John, owner & occupier,
merchant, Wolfe St.;
John McIver, occu-
pier, King St.; Paton
& Butcher, occupier,
Fairfax St.; Paton &
Batcher, occupier,
King St.;Capt. Sweet,
occupier, Royal St.

BUTT
Adam, occupier; Capt.
John Harper, owner,
Prince St.

CAMPBELL
James, occupier, mariner;
Dennis Ramsay, owner,
Fairfax St.

CARSON
John, occupier; William
Hodgson, owner, Fair-
fax St.

CARVILLE
Peter, occupier; William
Hunter, Sr., owner,
Fairfax St.

CASSONOVE
Peter, owner; John Potts,
occupier, King St.

5

CATON
Mary, occupier; Dennis
   Ramsay, owner, Royal
   St.

CAVERLY
Joseph, owner & occupier,
   Washington St.; owner
   & occupier, Wolfe St.
Peter, owner & occupier,
   Union St.

CHAMBERLIN
Hannah, occupier; Samuel
   Arell, owner, Duke
   St.

CHAPIN
Gurden, occupier,
   cashier-bank officer;
   William Hartshorne,
   owner, King St.
Margaret, owner & occu-
   pier, Fairfax St.

CHAPMAN
George, owner; Eliz.
   Hill, occupier, Duke
   St.

CHATHAM
James, occupier, black-
   smith; Samuel Arell,
   owner, Duke St.

CHEVALIER
Mrs., occupier; Mary Bur-
   nett, owner, Love
   Alley

CHEW
Roger, owner & occupier,
   Fairfax St.; Dykes

CHEW (continued)
   Fleming & Co., occu-
   pier, Fairfax St.;
   William Taylor, occu-
   pier, Fairfax St.

CLARKE
Richard, occupier; Thomas
   Gilpin (heirs),
   owner, Water St.

CLIFFORD
Jeremiah, owner & occu-
   pier, Princess St.
Nehemiah, owner; Fredk
   Shoemaker, occupier,
   Princess St.

COLEMAN
James, owner & occupier,
   Union St.; occupier,
   William Hartshorne,
   owner, Fairfax St.

CONN
Philip, owner & occupier,
   shop keeper, Pitt St.

CONWAY
occupier; John Fitz-
   gerald, owner, King
   St.
Richard, owner and occu-
   pier, Oronoka St.;
   Wm. Lowrey & Co.,
   occupier, Wharf;
   Joseph Thornton,
   occupier, Water St.;
   William Wilson, occu-
   pier, Wharf

COOK
Lewis, owner & occupier,
   bricklayer &
   stonemason, Pitt St.

COOPER
Elizabeth, owner; Jasper
   Isciloan, occupier,
   Cameron St.;
   Swillers, Hawke &
   Bonne, occupier,
   Union St.
George, occupier; Thomas
   Reed, owner, Queen
   St.
Jack (estate), owner;
   Andrew Runtzel, occu-
   pier, Fairfax St.

COPPER
Thomas, occupier,
mariner; Eliz. Flemming,
   owner, Union St.

CORYELL
George, owner & occupier,
   merchant, joiner,
   Duke St.

COUPER
Robert, occupier; Dennis
   Ramsay, owner,
   Fairfax St.

COX
Jacob, owner & occupier,
   tobacconist, gentle-
   man, Wilkes St.;
   Thomas Maservey,
   occupier, Fairfax St.

CRAIK
James, occupier, doctor;
   Capt. John Harper,
   owner, Prince St.

CRANDELL
Thomas, occupier, baker;
   Robert Adam (estate),
   owner, on the wharf;
   occupier, John Boyer,
   owner, Union St.;
   occupier, Christian
   Slimmer, owner, Union
   St.

CROWE
Lanty, occupier; William
   Bird, owner, Fairfax
   St.

DARLING & EARPS
occupier; Caleb Earps,
   owner, King St.

DAVIS
Samuel, owner & occupier,
   shipmaster, near
   Fairfax St.

DAVY
David, occupier,
   merchant; Peter Wise,
   owner, King St.

DAWE
Philip, owner; Porter &
   Ingraham, occupier,
   Fairfax St.

DEMPSTER
Hugh, occupier; Joseph
   Gilpin (heirs),
   owner, Union St.

DENEALE
Geo, owner & occupier,
   clerk, Duke St.

DICK
E.C., occupier, doctor;
   John Wise, owner,
   Royal St.

DILL
Richard Weightman, owner,
   Princess St.

DONALDSON
Robert, occupier; William
   Hartshorne, owner,
   Prince St.

DOUGHERTY
Robert, occupier; Thomas
   Reed, owner, Queen
   St.

DOUGLASS
James, occupier; Alexan-
   der Smith, owner,
   King St.

DUFFY
Barth, occupier; Hepburn
   & Dundass, owner,
   King St.
John, occupier, comb-
   maker; Richard Arell,
   owner, Royal St.

DUNCAN
George (estate), owner;
   Mich'l Madden, occu-
   pier, near Royal

DUNLAP & CRAIGE
occupier; Capt. John Har-
   per, owner, Fairfax
   St.

DUNN
Mrs., occupier; Peter
   Wise, owner, King St.

DUVALL
William, owner & occu-
   pier, Fairfax St.;
   Charles Lee, occu-
   pier, Cameron St.

DYKES FLEMING & CO.
occupier; Roger Chew,
   owner, Fairfax St.

DYKES
Mungo, owner & occupier,
   carpenter, Fairfax
   St.

EARPS
Caleb, owner, shopkeeper;
   Darling & Earps,
   occupier, King St.

EBHART
Adam, occupier; Peter
   Wise, owner, King
   St. with tan yard.

EDMUNDS
Edmond, occupier, school-
   master; William Her-
   bert, owner, near
   Fairfax

ELLIS (heirs)
owner; George Hill, occu-
   pier, near Water St.

8

FARREL
Wm., occupier, captain,
    mariner; Richard
    Arell, owner, Fairfax
    St.; occupier, John
    Wise, owner, Royal
    St.

FAUCET
John, occupier,
    blacksmith; William
    Wright, owner, Wilkes
    St.

FENDALL
Philip R., owner &
    occupier, Oronoka St.

FERGUSON
Cumb., owner & occupier,
    boarding house,
    Hooe's wharf.

FITZGERALD
John, owner & occupier,
    Naval officer, 5 Wolf
    St., Hill Houses;
    Conway, occupier,
    King St.; occupier,
    Bridget Kirk, owner,
    Wolf St.; owner,
    Nicholson & Co., oc-
    cupier, Fairfax St.;
    owner, 2 properties,
    William Wilson, occu-
    pier, Fairfax St.

FLEMING, DYKES & CO.
    occupier; Roger Chew,
    owner, Fairfax St.

FLEMING
Eliz., owner & occupier,
    Duke St.; Thomas Cop-
    per, occupier, Union
    St.; Richard Jenkins,
    occupier, Water St.

FLETCHER
James, owner & occupier,
    plaisterer, Wilkes
    St.

FORTNEY
Jacob, owner & occupier,
    King St.

FOUSHEE
John, owner & occupier,
    pilot, near Adam's
    Wharf

FOWLER
George (estate), owner;
    Ralph Longdon, occu-
    pier, Fairfax St.

FROUD
Mary, occupier; William
    Ramsay (estate),
    owner, near Royal St.

FULMORE
Joseph, owner & occupier,
    carpenter, St. Asaph
    St.

FULTON
Robert, owner & occupier,
    carpenter, Fairfax
    St.

GILPIN
George, owner & occupier,
    merchant, Union St.;
    occupier, William
    Hartshorne, owner,
    Prince St.
Joseph (heirs), owner;
    Hugh Dempster, occu-
    pier, Union St.; John
    Winterbury, occupier,
    Water St.
Thos. (heirs), owner;
    Richard Clarke, occu-
    pier, Water St.;
    Shreve and Lawrason,
    occupiers, Union St.

GOODES
George, owner and
    occupier, ship
    builder, Wolf St.

GOODS
Sam'l, occupier, ship
    builder; John Borer,
    owner, Water St.

GORDON
Alexander, owner and
    occupier, merchant
    shopkeeper, near King
    St.

GRAHAM
John, owner and occupier,
    Fairfax St.

GRAY
Anna, occupier, laborer;
    Capt. John Harper,
    owner, Prince St.

GREEN
Levi, occupier; Samuel
    Simmonds, owner,
    Royal St.

GREENWAY
Joseph, occupier; George
    Slacum, owner, Wilks
    St.

GRETTER
Eliz., owner and occu-
    pier, King St.
John, owner and occupier,
    King St.
Michael, owner; William
    Young, occupier,
    Queen St.; no one
    listed as occupier,
    Love Alley

HAGERTY
Patrick, occupier; Hep-
    burn and Dundass,
    owner, Oronoka St.

HALE
George, owner and occu-
    pier, cooper, brick-
    layer, Duke St.

HALL
Jonathan (heirs), owner;
    no one listed as oc-
    cupier, Water St.;
    Shreve & Lawrason,
    occupier, Union St.

10

HALLEY
William, occupier, mill-
stone maker; Eliz.
Parsons, owner, Fair-
fax St.

HAMP
Benjamin A., occupier;
Edward Ramsay, owner,
King St.

HAMPSON & WILLIAMS
occupier, Bryan Hampson
merchant; Adam L.
Swope, owner, Prince
St.

HANNAH
Negro, occupier; Josiah
Watson, owner, Pitt
St.
Nicholas, owner and
occupier, Capt. in
the U.S. Army, Common
Council Member, Duke
St.
Thos., occupier; Rober
Adam (estate), owner,
Queen St.

HANSON & BOND
occupier; Thomas
Williams, owner,
Prince St.

HANSON
Samuel, owner and occu-
pier, St. Asaph

HARLE
Robert, owner and occu-
pier, Royal St.; no
one listed as occu-

HARLE (continued)
pier, near Royal St.

HARPER
Hannah, occupier; Josiah
Watson, owner, Prince
St.
John, Capt., owner; Adam
Butt, occupier,
Prince St.; James
Craik, occupier,
Prince St.; Dunlap
and Craige, occupier,
Fairfax St.; Anna
Gray, occupant,
Prince St.; William
Hodgson, occupier,
Prince St.; James
McReady, occupier,
Prince St.; John Rey-
nolds, occupier,
Prince St.; Thomas
Vowele, occupier,
Prince St.; William
Young, occupier,
Prince St.
John, owner and occupier,
taylor, King St.;
occupier, Hepburn and
Dundass, owner, Pitt
St.
Sam'l, owner and
occupier, merchant,
near Wolfe St.
William, owner and
occupier, carpenter,
Wolf St.

HARRISON
Robert H. (estate),
owner; Michael Pep-
per, occupier, Water
St.; Levi Talbot,

11

HARRISON (continued)
occupier, Water St.
Sam'l, owner; Richard
Weightman, occupier,
Fairfax St.; owner &
occupier, King St.

HARROW
Gilbert, occupier; John
Muir, owner, Duke St.

HARTSHORNE & DONALDSON
occupier; William
Hartshorne, owner,
Hooe's Wharf; William
Hartshorne, owner,
Kirk's Wharf

HARTSHORNE
William, owner; Gurden
Chapin, occupier,
King St.; James Cole-
man, occupier, Fair-
fax St.; Robert
Donaldson, occupier,
Prince St.; George
Gilpin, occupier,
Prince St.;
Hartshorne and
Donaldson, occupier,
Kirk's Wharf; Hart-
shorne and Donaldson,
occupier, Hooe's
Wharf; George Taylor,
occupier, Prince St.

HAWKINS
John, occupier; William
Baker, owner, Fairfax
St.

HAYES
Andrew, owner and
occupier, sadler,
Prince St.

HEIDIE
occupier; Michael Thorn,
owner, Near Union

HEINEMAN
Jacob, owner and
occupier, Washington
St.

HEPBURN & DUNDASS
owner and occupier, 2
properties, King St.;
Bartholemew Duffy,
occupier, King St.;
Patrick Hagerty,
occupier, Oronoka
St.; John Harper,
occupier, Pitt St.;
Arthur Lee, occupier,
Princess St.; James
McKenna, occupier,
King St.; Massett,
occupier, Union St.

HENLY
David, owner; William
McWhir, occupier,
Wolfe St.; John
Mortland, occupier,
Duke St.

HERBERT
Thomas, owner; John Wise,
occupier, Fairfax St.
William, owner and occu-
pier, near Fairfax;
Washer Blunt, occu-
pier, Water St.;

12

HERBERT (continued)
    Edmond Edmunds, occu-
      pier, near Fairfax;
      R.B. Jamieson, occu-
      pier, near Fairfax;
      Neil Mooney, occu-
      pier, Oronoka St.

HERBERT & POTTS
owner; Levi Talbot, occu-
    pier, near Royal St.

HESSHUYSEN
occupier; John Wise,
    owner, Fairfax St.

HEWES
Aaron, owner and
    occupier, Hatter,
    Prince St.

HICKMAN
William, owner and occu-
    pier, merchant, St.
    Asaph; occupier, John
    Muir, owner, King St.

HIKER
Henry, occupier; Patrick
    Allison, owner, King
    St.

HILL
Eliza., occupier; George
    Chapman, owner, Duke
    St.
George, occupier, cooper;
    Ellis (heirs),
    owners, near Water
    St.

HODGSON
William, owner and occu-
    pier, merchant, Water
    St.; occupier, Robert
    Adam (estate), owner,
    on the Wharf; John
    Carson, occupier,
    Fairfax St.; occu-
    pier, Capt. John
    Harper, owner, Prince
    St.; William Lowry
    and Company, occu-
    pier, Prince St.;
    occupier, John Wise,
    owner, Prince St.

HOOE
Robert T, owner, mer-
    chant; Hooe and Har-
    rison, occupier,
    Wharf; Hooe and Har-
    rison, occupier,
    Prince St.; Catharine
    Spicott, occupier,
    Wharf

HOOE & HARRISON
occupier; Robert T
    Hooe, owner, Prince
    St.; occupier, Robert
    T Hooe, owner, Wharf

HOOFF
Lawrence, owner and occu-
    pier, King St.;
    William Keech, occu-
    pier, King St.;
    Bushrod Washington,
    occupier, Duke St.
Margaret, owner; Rogerson
    and Dabney, occupier,
    Fairfax St.

HOWARD
   occupier; James Lawra-
   son, owner, Fairfax
   St.

HUGHES
John, occupier,
   shipbuilder; Michael
   Thorn, owner, near
   Union

HUNTER
George, owner and
   occupier, Fairfax St.
John, owner and occupier,
   ship carpenter,
   builder, Fairfax St.
John Chapman, owner;
   William Wilson, occu-
   pier, Duke St.
Nathaniel, owner; Tatsa-
   paw, occupier, Fair-
   fax St.
William, occupier; Dennis
   Ramsay, owner, Water
   St.
William, Jr., owner and
   occupier, alderman,
   Union St.; owner and
   occupier, Fairfax
   St.; Charles Bell,
   occupier, Queen St.;
   Henry Budd, occupier,
   Prince St.; Mrs. Pey-
   ton, occupier, Wilkes
   St.
William, Sr., owner;
   William Bryce, occu-
   pier, Union St.;
   Peter Carville, occu-
   pier, Fairfax St.;
   Ludwel Lee, occupier,
   Wilkes St.

IRVINE
Thomas, occupier, mer-
   chant; Benjamin
   Shreve, owner, Fair-
   fax St.

ISCILOAN
Jasper, occupier; Eliza-
   beth Cooper, owner,
   Cameron St.

JACKSON
David (heirs), owner;
   William Morgan, occu-
   pier, Fairfax St.

JAMIESON
R.B., occupier; William
   Herbert, owner, near
   Fairfax

JANNEY
Joseph, owner, merchant;
   Merryman and Green,
   occupier, Fairfax
   St.; Nathan'l
   Spooner, occupier,
   Wolf St.

JENCKES WINSOR & COMPANY
owner; Olney Winsor,
   occupier, King St.

JENKINS
Richard, occupier; Eliza-
   beth Fleming, owner,
   Water St.

KIMBO
John, occupier; William
   Ramsay (estate),
   owner, near Royal St.

KING
Suky, occupier; Robert
Adam (estate), owner,
Fairfax St.

KIRK
Bridget, owner; John
Fitzgerald, occupier,
Wolf St.

KIRKPATRICK
Thos. (estate), owner;
Brown, occupier,
Water St.; William
Wools, occupier,
Water St.

KEAN
John, occupier; William
Bird, owner, Fairfax
St.

KEECH
William, occupier;
Lawrence Hooff,
owner, King St.

KEITH
James, owner and
occupier, Water St.

KNOWER
Andrew, occupier; Hannah
Bryce, owner, Prince
St.

KORN
John, owner and occupier,
baker, Prince St.

KORN & WEISMILLER
occupier; Jacob
Weismiller, owner,

KORN & WEISMILLER (cont)
St. Asaph

KURTZ
Nicholas, occupier; Anna
Lake, owner, King St.

LAKE
Anna, owner and occupier,
King St.; Nicholas
Kurtz, occupier, King
St.

LANGSTON
Benjamin, occupier,
printer; William
Bushby, owner, near
Duke St.

LARKIN
Joseph, occupier; Samuel
Simmonds, owner,
Fairfax St

LATTIMORE
Harry, occupier; Robert
Adam (estate), owner,
near Princess St.

LAWRASON
James, owner and occu-
pier, merchant, St.
Asaph; Howard, occu-
pier, Fairfax St.;
occupier, Shreve and
Lawrason, owner, St.
Asaph

LEE
Arthur, occupier; Hepburn
and Dundass, owner,
Princess St. (corner
of Water and

15

LEE (continued)
   Princess)
Charles, owner and occu-
   pier, Queen St.;
   occupier, William
   Duvall, owner,
   Cameron St.
Ludwel, occupier; William
   Hunter, Sr., owner,
   Wilkes St.

LOMAX
John (estate), owner;
   Joseph Thomas, occu-
   pier

LONGDON
John, owner and occupier,
   taylor, Royal St.
Ralph, occupier; George
   Fowler (estate), own-
   er, Fairfax St.

LOWNES
James, occupier; Michael
   Madden, owner, Prince
   St.

LOWREY
Wm. and Co., occupier;
   Richard Conway,
   owner, Wharf;
   occupier, William
   Hodgson, owner,
   Prince St.; occupier,
   Robert Lyle (estate),
   owner, Fairfax St.

LUTZ
Michael, owner and
   occupier, tanner,
   Wilkes St.

LYLE
Robert, owner and
   occupier, Queen St.
Robert (estate), owner;
   no one named as occu-
   pant, Alley; Anderson
   and Jamieson, occu-
   pier, Royal St.;
   William Lowrey, occu-
   pier, Fairfax St.;
   John Pettit, occu-
   pier, Fairfax St.

LYNN
Adam (estate), owner;
   Lynn and Walden,
   occupier, King St.

LYNN & WALDEN
occupier; Adam Lynn
   (estate), owner, King
   St.

McBRIDE
William, occupier;
   Richard Arell, owner,
   Fairfax St.

McCLANAHAN
John, owner and occupier,
   Union St.; owner and
   occupier, Prince St.

McCREA
Robert, owner and occu-
   pier, Royal St.; John
   McIver, occupier,
   Union St.; Mrs. Mann,
   occupier, alley near
   Union St.

McCUE
Henry, occupier, drayman;
    Richard Arell, owner,
    Royal St.

McGAHEN
Hugh, owner and occupier,
    Fairfax St.

McHENRY
James, owner and occu-
    pier, Princess St.

McIVER
John, occupier; John
    Butcher, owner, King
    St.; occupier, Robert
    McCrea, owner, Union
    St.; Shuttle, occu-
    pier, Fairfax St.

McKENNA
James, occupier, bank
    officer; Hepburn and
    Dundass, owner, King
    St.

McKNAB
Thomas, occupier; William
    Bushby, owner, Fair-
    fax St.

McKNIGHT
William, owner and occu-
    pier, King St.;
    owner, John
    Mandeville, occupier,
    King St.

McLEAN
Samuel, owner; William
    Shakespeare, occu-
    pier, Queen St.

McLIESH
James, owner and occu-
    pier, Union St.

McPHERSON
Daniel and Isaac, owner
    and occupier, Prince
    St.; occupier, John
    Saunders (estate),
    owner, Prince St.;
    Isaac, occupier, mer-
    chant, John Warder
    (Philadelphia),
    owner, King St.

McREADY
James, occupier; Capt.
    John Harper, owner,
    Prince St.

McWHIR
William, occupier; David
    Henly, owner, Wolfe
    St.

MADDEN
Michael, owner; Patrick
    Burns, occupier,
    Prince St.; occupier,
    George Duncan
    (estate), owner, near
    Royal St.; owner,
    James Lownes, occu-
    pier, Prince St.

MANDEVILLE
John, owner and occupier,
    Queen St.; occupier,
    William McKnight,
    owner, King St.

17

MANN
Mrs., occupier; Robert
  McCrea, owner, Alley
  near Union
Bernhard, owner and
  occupier, drayman,
  Water St.

MARKS
William, occupier,
  sadler; Richard
  Arell, owner, Fairfax
  St.

MARR
Peggy, Mrs., occupier,
  seamstress; Andrew
  Wales, owner, Fairfax
  St.

MARSTELLER
Philip, owner and
  occupier, Mayor,
  merchant, Water St.

MASERVEY
Thos., occupier,
  shopkeeper; Jacob
  Cox, owner, Fairfax
  St.

MASSETT
occupier; Hepburn and
  Dundass, owner, Union
  St.

MERRYMAN & GREENE
occupier; Joseph Janney,
  owner, Fairfax St.

MILLER
Mordecai, occupier,
  silversmith,

MILLER (continued)
  watchmaker; Benj.
  Shreve, owner,
  Fairfax St.

MOLDS
Ann, occupier; Richard
  Bond, owner, Fairfax
  St.

MOONEY
Neil, occupier; William
  Bond, owner, Oronoka
  St.

MOORE
Cleon, owner and
  occupier, Notary
  Public, St. Asaph

MORGAN
occupier; Dennis Ramsay,
  owner, Queen St.
William, occupier; David
  Jackson (heirs),
  owner, Fairfax St.

MORTLAND
John, occupier; David
  Henly, owner, Duke
  St.

MUIR
John, owner and occupier,
  King St.; owner, no
  one listed as occu-
  pant, Royal St.; John
  Beale, occupier, King
  St.; Gilbert Harrow,
  occupier, Duke St.;
  William Hickman,
  occupier, King St.
Robert (heirs), owner;

MUIR (continued)
John Paisley, occu-
pier, King St.

MULLIKIN
John, owner and occupier,
2 properties, Oronoka
St.

MURRAY
John, owner and occupier,
alderman, Prince St.
John, occupier; Lewis
Weston, owner, Water
St.
Patrick, owner and
occupier, Prince St.

NEWMAN
Ann, occupier; William
Bushby, owner,
Fairfax St.

NEWTON
William, occupier,
merchant; Alexander
Smith, owner, King
St.

NICHOLS
Eli, owner; Absolom Rowe,
occupier, near Wilkes
St.
Isaac, owner; William
Rhodes, occupier,
near Fairfax St.

NICHOLSON & CO.
occupier; John Fitz-
gerald, owner, Fair-
fax St.

NORRIS
William, occupier;
Morriss Worrell,
owner, near Royal St.

PAGE
William, occupier; Andrew
Wales, owner, Union
St.

PAISLEY
John, occupier; Robert
Muir (heirs), owner,
King St.

PANCOAST
David (estate), owner;
Henry Walker, occu-
pier, St. Asaph St.

PARSONS
Elizabeth, owner and
occupier, Cameron
St.; William Halley,
occupier, Fairfax St.

PATON
William, owner and
occupier, merchant,
common council
member, Pitt St.

PATON & BUTCHER
occupier; John Butcher,
owner, Fairfax St.;
occupier, John
Butcher, owner, King
St.; occupier, Benj.
Shreve, owner, Fair-
fax St.

PATTERSON
William, occupier; James
    Wright, owner, Queen
    St.

PEPPER
Michael, occupier; Robert
    H Harrison (estate),
    owner, Water St.

PERRIN
Joseph M., owner and
    occupier, Royal St.

PERRY
Alexander, owner and
    occupier, Fairfax St.

PETTIT
John, owner and occupier
    King St.; occupier,
    Robert Lyle (estate),
    owner, Fairfax St.

PEYTON
Mrs., occupier; William
    Hunter, Jr., owner,
    Wilkes St.
Francis, owner and occu-
    pier, King St.; occu-
    pier, Richard Rat-
    cliff, owner, St.
    Asaph

PHERNO
Philip, owner and
    occupier, St Asaph
    St.

PILE
Peter, occupier,
    tobacconist; Richard
    Arell, owner, Royal

PILE (continued)
    St.

POLLY
occupier; William Bushby,
    owner, Near Fairfax
    St.

PORTER
Thomas, owner, common
    council member;
    William Ward, occu-
    pier, Royal St.

PORTER & INGRAHAM
occupier; Philip Dawe,
    owner, Fairfax St.

POTTS
John, occupier; Peter
    Cassonove, owner,
    King St.

POULTNEY
Thomas, occupier; Thomas
    Williams, owner,
    Royal St.

PRICE
Oliver, owner and occu-
    pier, Fairfax St.;
    Valentine Uhler,
    occupier, St. Asaph
    St.

QUEENBREAD
William, owner and
    occupier, Prince St.

RAMSAY
Amelia, owner; William
    Ward, occupier, Royal
    St.

RAMSAY (continued)
Dennis, owner and occu-
    pier, alderman, Fair-
    fax St.; James
    Campbell, occupier,
    Fairfax St.; Mary
    Caton, occupier,
    Royal St.; Robert
    Couper, occupier,
    Fairfax St.; William
    Hunter, occupier,
    Water St.; Morgan,
    occupier, Queen St.
Edward, owner; Benjamin A
    Hamp, occupier, King
    St.
William, owner and
    occupier, Fairfax St.
William (estate), owner;
    Mary Froud, occupier,
    near Royal St.; John
    Kimbo, occupier, near
    Royal St.

RATCLIFF
Richard, owner; John
    Beatis, occupier, St.
    Asaph St.; Francis
    Peyton, occupier, St.
    Asaph St.

REDMAN
Thomas, owner and
    occupier, ordinary
    keeper, Prince St.

REED
Thomas, owner and occu-
    pier, Queen St.;
    George Cooper, occu-
    pier, Queen St.;
    Robert Dougherty,
    occupier, Queen St.

REEVES
Leonard, occupier,
    bricklayer; Michael
    Thorn, owner, Near
    Union St.

RESLER
Jacob, occupier,
    chandler; Betty
    Steuart owner, Royal
    St.

REYNOLDS
John, owner and occupier,
    Naval officer, Prin-
    cess St.; occupier,
    Capt. John Harper,
    owner, Prince St.
Michael, occupier; Josiah
    Watson, owner,
    Fairfax St.

RHODES
William, owner and occu-
    pier, Fairfax St.;
    occupier, Isaac
    Nichols, owner, near
    Fairfax St.

RICHARDS
Thomas, owner; George
    Rutter, occupier,
    Prince St.

RICKS
William, occupier; Andrew
    Wales, owner, Fairfax
    St.

RIGG
John, owner and occupier,
    bricklayer, Royal St.

21

ROBERDEAU
Daniel, owner and occu-
pier, schoolmaster,
Water St.

ROGERSON & DABNEY
occupier, merchants;
Margaret Hooff,
owner, Fairfax St.

ROWE
Absolom, occupier,
shipbuilder,
wharfbuilder; Eli
Nichols, owner, Near
Wilkes St.

RUNTZEL
Andrew, occupier,
blacksmith; Jack
Cooper (estate),
owner, Fairfax St.

RUTTER
George, occupier,
shopkeeper,
innkeeper; Thomas
Richards, owner,
Prince St.

SANFORD
Catharine, owner and
occupier, Fairfax St.
Edward, owner and occu-
pier, silversmith,
St. Asaph St.

SAUNDERS
John (estate), owner;
Daniel and Isaac
McPherson, occupier,
Prince St.; William
Saunders, occupier,

SAUNDERS (continued)
Prince St.
William, occupier; John
Saunders (estate),
owner, Prince St.

SHAKESPEARE
William, occupier; Samuel
McLean, owner, Queen
St.

SHAW
Eleazor, owner and
occupier, Queen St.

SHOEMAKER
Fred'k, occupier;
Nehemiah Clifford,
owner, Princess St.

SHORTLEY
Luke, occupier,
carpenter; Josiah
Watson, owner, Water
St.

SHREVE
Benjamin, owner and occu-
pier, common council
member, merchant,
King St.; Thomas
Irvine, occupier,
Fairfax St.; Mordecai
Miller, occupier,
Fairfax St.; Paton
and Butcher, occu-
pier, Fairfax St.

SHREVE & LAWRASON
owner and occupier, 2
properties, Union
St.; occupier, Thomas
Gilpin (heirs),

SHREVE & LAWRASON (cont)
owners, Union St.;
occupier, Jonathan
Hall (heirs), owners,
Union St.; owner,
James Lawrason, occu-
pier, St. Asaph St.

SHUCK
Jacob, owner and occu-
pier, carpenter, Duke
St.; John Stokes,
occupier, Duke St.

SHUGARTS
Zachariah, owner and
occupier, Water St.

SHUTTLE
occupier; John McIver,
owner, Fairfax St.

SIMM
Robert, occupier; Thomas
West, owner, Princess
St.

SIMMONDS
Samuel, owner and occu-
pier, shoemaker,
Fairfax St.; Levi
Green, occupier,
Royal St.; Joseph
Larkin, occupier,
Fairfax St.

SIMMS
Charles, owner and
occupier, attorney
lawyer, Pitt St.

SLACUM
Gabriel, owner; Selbourn
Williams, occupier,
Wilkes St.
George, owner, mariner,
shipmaster; Joseph
Greenway, occupier,
Wilkes St.

SLIMMER
Christian, owner and
occupier,
housekeeper, Water
St.; Thomas Crandell,
occupier, Union St.

SMITH
Alexander, owner,
inspector, merchant;
James Douglass, occu-
pier, King St.;
William Newton, occu-
pier, King st.; occu-
pier, Andrew Wales,
owner, Water St.
Daniel, occupier; Peter
Wise, owner, King St.
John, owner and occupier,
Washington St.

SPANGLER
Baltzer, owner; A.L.
Swope, occupier,
Prince St.

SPICOTT
Catharine, occupier;
Robert T. Hooe,
owner, Wharf

SPOONER
Nathaniel, occupier,
mariner; Joseph

SPOONER (continued)
Janney, owner, Wolfe
St.

STEUART
Betty, owner and occu-
pier, King St.; James
Balfour, occupier,
King St.; Resler,
occupier, Royal St.
John, owner and occupier,
cabinet maker, Prince
St.

STEER
Adam, occupier; William
Bushby, owner,
Fairfax St.

STIEBER
Michael, owner and
occupier, baker,
Royal St.

STOKES
John, occupier; Jacob
Shuck, owner, Duke
St.

STRAYER & HEIDE
owner and occupier,
Prince St.

STROWMAN
Henry, owner and
occupier, Royal St.

SULLIVAN
John, owner and occupier,
bricklayer, Water St.

SUMMERS
William, owner and

SUMMERS (continued)
occupier, Prince St.

SUTTON
John, owner and occupier,
Royal St.

SWEET
Capt., occupier; John
Butcher, owner, Royal
St.

SWIFT
Jonathan, owner and
occupier, Fairfax St.

SWILLERS, HAWKE, & BOONE
occupier, Joseph
Swellor, taylor,
Elizabeth Cooper,
owner, Union St.

SWOPE
Adam L., owner, merchant;
Hampson and Williams
occupier, Prince St.
A.L., occupier; Baltzer
Spangler, owner,
Prince St.

TALBOT
Mrs., occupier; Robert
Adam (estate), owner,
Queen St.
Levi, occupier; Robert H.
Harrison (estate),
owner, Water St.;
occupier, Herbert and
Potts, owner, near
Royal St.

TATSAPAW
Adam, occupier,

TATSAPAW (continued)
carpenter; Nathaniel
Hunter, owner,
Fairfax St.
Peter, owner and
occupier, carpenter,
Fairfax St.

TAYLOR
George, occupier,
merchant; William
Hartshorne, owner,
Prince St.
Jesse, owner and
occupier, alderman,
merchant, Pitt and
King St.
William, occupier; Roger
Chew, owner, Fairfax
St.

THOMAS
Joseph, occupier; John
Lomax (estate),
owner, Princess St.

THOMPSON
Edward K., owner and
occupier, Prince St.;
occupier, Richard W.
Ashton, owner, Water
St.
Jonah, occupier,
merchant; Richard
Arell, owner, King
St.

THORN
Michael, owner and occu-
pier, Prince St.;
Heide, occupier, near
Union St.; Hughes,
occupier, near Union

THORN (continued)
St.; Reeves, occu-
pier, near Union St.

THORNTON
Joseph, occupier, baker,
shopkeeper; Richard
Conway, owner, Water
St.

UHLER
Valentine, occupier,
sadler; Oliver Price,
owner

VOWELL
Thomas, occupier, mer-
chant; Capt. John
Harper, owner, Prince
St.; occupier, Peter
Wise, owner, Fairfax
St.

WALES
Andrew, owner and occu-
pier, brewer, near
Water St.; Mrs. Mary,
occupier, Fairfax
St.; William Page,
occupier, Union St.;
William Ricks, occu-
pier, Fairfax St.;
Andrew Smith, occu-
pier, Water St.

WALKER
Henry, occupier,
schoolmaster; David
Pancoast (estate),
owner, St. Asaph St.

WARD
William, occupier; Thomas

25

WARD (continued)
Porter, owner, Royal St.; occupier, Amelia Ramsay, owner, Royal St.

WARDER
John (Philadelphia), owner; Isaac McPherson, occupier, King St.

WARDEN
William, owner and occupier, Cameron St.

WASHINGTON
Bushrod, owner and occupier, Wolf St.; occupier, Lawrence Hooff, owner, Duke St.

WATSON
Josiah, owner and occupier, merchant, Pitt St.; owner and occupier, Union St.; owner, Bozwell, occupier, Fairfax St.; Negro Hannah, occupier, Pitt St.; Hannah Harper, occupier, Prince St.; Michael Reynolds, occupier, Fairfax St.; Luke Shortley, occupier, Water St.

WEBSTER
Philip, owner and occupier, St. Asaph St.

WEIGHTMAN
Richard, owner, taylor; Dill, occupier, Princess St.; occupier, Samuel Harrison, owner, Fairfax St.

WEISMILLER
Jacob, owner; Korn and Weismiller, occupier, St. Asaph St.

WEST
Thomas, owner and occupier, Prince St.; Robert Simm, occupier, Princess St.

WESTON
Lewis, owner and occupier, Water St.; John Murray, occupier, Water St.

WHITE
Thomas, occupier; Robert Adam (estate), owner, Fairfax St.

WILKINSON
Thomas, owner and occupier, Fairfax St.

WILLIAMS
Selbourn, occupier; Gabriel Slacum, owner, Wilkes St.
Thomas, owner, merchant; Hanson and Bond, occupier, Prince St.; Thomas Poultney, occupier, Royal St.

WILSON
James, occupier,
  merchant; Peter Wise,
  owner, King St.
William, occupier,
  carpenter; Richard
  Conway, owner, Wharf;
  occupier, 2 proper-
  ties; John Fitz-
  gerald, owner, Fair-
  fax St.; occupier;
  John Chapman Hunter,
  owner, Duke St.

WINSOR
Olney, occupier,
  recorder; Jenckes
  Winson and Co.,
  owner, King St.

WINTERBURY
John, occupier,
  shoemaker; Joseph
  Gilpin (heirs),
  owner, Water St.

WISE
John, owner, sadler; E.
  C. Dick, occupier,
  Royal St.; William
  Farrel, occupier,
  Royal St.; occupier,
  Thomas Herbert,
  owner, Fairfax St.;
  owner, Hesshuysen,
  occupier, Fairfax
  St.; William Hodgson,
  occupier, Prince St.
Peter, owner and occu-
  pier, common council
  member, King St.;
  David Davy, occupier,
  King St.; Mrs. Dunn,

WISE (continued)
  occupier, King St.;
  Adam Ebhart, occu-
  pier, King St. with
  tanyard; Daniel
  Smith, occupier, King
  St.; Thomas Vowell,
  occupier, Fairfax
  St.; James Wilson,
  occupier, King St.

WOOLS
William, occupier; Thomas
  Kirkpatrick (estate),
  owner, Water St.

WORRELL
Morriss, owner and occu-
  pier, carpenter, near
  Royal; William
  Norris, occupier,
  near Royal St.

WRIGHT
James, owner; William
  Patterson, occupier,
  Queen St.
William, owner and occu-
  pier, stonecutter,
  bricklayer, Wilkes
  St.; no one listed as
  occupant, Prince St.;
  Faucet, occupier,
  Wilkes St.

YOST
John, owner & occupier,
  blacksmith, Fairfax
  St.

YOUNG
David, owner & occupier,
  Royal St.

YOUNG (continued)
William, occupier,
    Michael Gretter, own-
    er, Queen St.; occu-
    pier, Capt. John
    Harper, owner, Prince
    St.

SECOND PART

Distribution of Ownership
Alexandria, 1791

The listing below sets forth the distribution of ownership, street by street, in Alexandria in 1791. To determine whether the individual(s) listed under the street name(s) were the owner or the occupant of the property, refer to the FIRST PART.

Washington St. - 4 owners
St. Asaph St. - 14 owners
Pitt St. - 8 owners
Royal St. - 30 owners
Fairfax St. - 83 owners
Water St. - 33 owners
Union St. - 23 owners
Gibbon St. - 1 owner
Wilkes St. - 11 owners
Wolfe St. - 9 owners
Duke St. - 18 owners
Prince St. - 42 owners
King St. - 47 owners

Cameron St. - 5 owners
Queen St. - 15 owners
Princess St. - 9 owners
Oronoco St. - 5 owners

Wharfs:
(1) Hooe - 3 owners
(2) Conway - 1 owner
(3) Adams - 1 owner
     near Adams - 2 owners
     Kirks (not located)
     - 1 owner

ALLEY
Lyle, Robert

CAMERON
Allison, Patrick
Cooper, Elizabeth
Duvall, William
Isciloan (Jociloan),
     Jasper
Lee, Charles
Parsons, Elizabeth
Warden, William

DUKE
Arell, Richard
     Samuel

DUKE (continued)
Chamberlin, Hannah
Chatham, James

NEAR DUKE
Bushby, William
Langston

DUKE
Butt, Jacob
Chapman, George
Coryell, George
Deneale, George
Fitzpatrick, Thos.
Fleming, Elizabeth
Hale, George

29

DUKE (conninued)
Hannah Nicholas
Harrow, Gilbert
Henly, David
Hill, Elizabeth
Hooff, Lawrence
Hunter, John Chapman
Mortland, John
Muir, John
Shuck, Jacob
Stokes, John
Washington, Bushrod
Wilson, William

FAIRFAX
Adam, Robert (estate)
Arell, Richard
Baker, William
Bird, William
Bloss, Adam
Bond, Richard
Bright, John
Crowe, Lanty
Farrel, William
Hawkins, John
Kean, John
King, Suky
McBride, Wm.
Marks, William
Molds, Ann
White, Thos.

NEAR FAIRFAX
Bromley, William

FAIRFAX
Brown, William
Burns, John
Bushby, Joseph
    William

NEAR FAIRFAX
Allison, Elizabeth

NEAR FAIRFAX (cont)
Bushby, William

FAIRFAX
Bushby, William
McNab, Thomas
Newman, Ann

NEAR FAIRFAX
Bushby, William
Polly

FAIRFAX
Bushby, William
Butcher, John
Chapin, Margaret
Chew, Roger
Cooper, Jack (estate)
Cox, Jacob
Dykes Fleming & Co.
Maservey, Thos.
Paton & Butcher
Runtzel, Andrew
Steer, Adam
Taylor, William

NEAR FAIRFAX
David, Samuel

FAIRFAX
Coleman, James
Dawe, Philip
Dunlap & Craige
Duvall, William
Dykes, Mungo
Fitzgerald, John
Fowler, George (estate)
Fulton, Robert
Graham, John
Harper, Capt. John
Harrison, Samuel
Hartshorne, William
Herbert, Thomas

FAIRFAX (continued)
Langdon, Ralph
Nicholson & Co.
Porter & Ingraham
Weightman, Richard
Wilson, William
Wise, John

NEAR FAIRFAX
Herbert, William

FAIRFAX
Edmunds, Edmond
Herbert, William

NEAR FAIRFAX
Herbert, William
Jamieson, R. B.

FAIRFAX
Carson, John
Carville, Peter
Hodgson, William
Hooff, Margaret
Howard
Hunter, George
Hunter, John
    Nathaniel
    William Jr.
    William Sr.
Jackson, David (heirs)
Janney, Joseph
Lawrason, James
Lowrey, William
Lyle, Robert (estate)
McGahen, Hugh
McIver, John
Merryman and Green
Morgan, William
Pettit, John
Rogerson & Dabney
Shuttle
Tatsapaw

NEAR FAIRFAX
Nichols, Isaac
Rhodes, William

FAIRFAX
Bozwell
Campbell, James
Couper, Robert
Halley, William
Hesshuysen
Irvine, Thomas
Larkin, Joseph
Marr, Mrs.
Miller, Mordecai
Parsons, Eliz
Paton & Butcher
Perry, Alexander
Price, Oliver
Ramsay, Dennis
    William
Reynolds, Michael
Rhodes, William
Ricks, William
Sanford, Catherine
Shreve, Benjamin
Simmonds, Samuel
Swift, Jonathan
Tatsapaw, Peter
Vowell, Thomas
Wales, Andrew
Watson, Josiah
Wilkinson, Thomas
Wise, John
    Peter
Yost, John

NEAR GIBBON
Bence, Adam

KING
Allison, John
    Patrick
    Robert

31

KING (continued)
Anderson, Eliz.
   William
Arell, Richard
Bryan, Charles
Buchan & Patton
Butcher, John
Cassonove, Peter
Conway
Darling & Earps
Earps, Caleb
Fitzgerald, John
Fortney, Jacob
Hiker, Henry
McIver, John
Paton & Butcher
Potts, John
Thompson, Jonah

NEAR KING
Gordon, Alexander

KING
Balfour, James
Beale, John
Chapin, Gurden
Davy, David
Douglass, James
Duffy, Barth.
Dunn, Mrs.
Gretter, Elizabeth
   John
Hamp, Benjamin A.
Harper, John
Harrison, Saml
Hartshorne, William
Hepburn & Dundass
Hickman, William
Hooff, Lawrence
Jenckes Winsor & Co.
Keech, William
Kurtz, Nicholas
Lake, Anna

KING (continued)
Lynn, Adam (estate)
Lynn & Walden
McKenna, James
McKnight, William
McPherson, Isaac
Mandeville, John
Muir, John
   Robert (heirs)
Newton, William
Paisley, John
Pettit, John
Peyton, Frances
Ramsay, Edward
Shreve, Benjamin
Smith, Alexander
Steuart, Betty
Warden, John (Philadel-
   phia)
Winsor, Olney
Wise, Peter

KING WITH TANYARD
Erhart, Adam
Wise, Peter

KING
Smith, Daniel
Wilson, James
Wise, Peter

LOVE ALLEY
Burnett, Mary
Chevalier, Mrs.
Gretter, Michael

ORONOKA
Conway, Richard
Fendall, Philip R.
Hagerty, Patrick
Hepburn & Dundass
Herbert, William
Mooney, Neil

ORONOKA (continued)
Mullikin, John

NEAR PRINCE
Blunt, Washer

PRINCE
Bryce, Hannah
Budd, Henry
Burns, Patrick
Butt, Adam
Craik, James
Donaldson, Robert
Gilpin, George
Gray, Anna
Hampson & Wiliams
Hanson & Bond
Harper, Hannah
   Capt. John
Hartshorne, William
Hayes, Andrew
Hewes, Aaron
Hodgson, William
Hooe, Robert T.
Hooe & Harrison
Hunter, William Jr.
Knower, Andrew
Korn, John
Lownes, James
McClanahan, John
McPherson, Daniel & Isaac
McReady, James
Madden, Michael
Murray, John
   Patrick
Queenbread, William
Redman, Thomas
Reynolds, John
Richards, Thomas
Rutter, George
Saunder, John (estate)
Saunders, John (estate)
   Mrs.

PRINCE (continued)
Spangler, Baltzer
Steuart, John
Strayer and Heide
Summers, William
Swope, A. L.
Swope, Adam L.
Taylor, George
Thom, Michael
Thompson, Edward K.
Vowele, Thomas
Watson, Josiah
West, Thomas
Wm. Lowry & Co.
Williams, Thomas
Wise, John
Wright, William
Young, William

NEAR PRINCESS
Adam, Robert (estate)
Lattimore, Harry

PRINCESS
Clifford, Jeremiah
   Nehemiah
Dill
Hepburn & Dundass
Lee, Arthur
Lomax, John (estate)
McHenry, James
Reynolds, John
Shoemaker, Frdk
Simm, Robert
Thomas, Joseph
Weightman, Richard
West, Thomas

PITT
Conn, Philip
Cook, Lewis
Harper, John
Hepburn & Dundass

PITT (continued)
Paton, William
Simms, Charles

PITT & KING
Taylor, Jesse

PITT
Watson, Josiah
Hannah, Negro

QUEEN
Adam, Robert (estate)
Bell, Charles
Bloss, Adam
Cooper, George
Dougherty, Robert
Gretter, Michael
Hannah, Thos.
Hunter, William Jr.
Lee, Charles
Lyle, Robert
McLean, Samuel
Mandeville, John
Morgan
Patterson, William
Ramsay, Dennis
Reed, Thomas
Shakespeare, William
Shaw, Eleazor
Talbot, Mrs.
Wright, James
Young, William

ROYAL
Arell, Richard
Butcher, John
Duffy, John
McCue, Henry
Pile, Peter
Sweet, Capt.

NEAR ROYAL
Duncan, George (estate)
Madden, Michael

ROYAL
Harle, Robert

NEAR ROYAL
Harle, Robert

ROYAL
Herbert & Potts
Talbot, Levi

NEAR ROYAL
Longdon, John

ROYAL
Anderson & Jamieson
Caton, Mary
Lyle, Robert (estate)
McCrea, Robert
Muir, John
Perrin, Joseph M.
Porter, Thomas
Ramsay, Amelia
    Dennis
Ward, William

NEAR ROYAL
Froud, Mary
Kimbo, John
Ramsay, William (estate)

ROYAL
Dick, E. C.
Farrel, William
Green, Levi
Poultney, Thomas
Resler
Rigg, John
Simmonds, Samuel
Steuart, Betty

ROYAL (continued)
Stieber, Michael
Strowman, Henry
Sutton, John
Williams, Thomas
Wise, John
Worrell, Morriss

NEAR ROYAL
Norris, William
Worrell, Morriss

ROYAL
Young, David

ST. ASAPH
Beatis, John
Fulmore, Joseph
Hanson, Samuel
Hickman, William
Korn & Weismiller
Lawrason, James
Moore, Cleon
Pancoast, David (estate)
Peyton, Francis
Pherno, Philip
Price, Oliver
Ratcliff, Richard
Sanford, Edward
Shreve & Lawrason
Uhler, Valentine
Walker, Henry
Webster, Philip
Weismiller, Jacob

UNION
Boyer, John
Bryce, William
Caverly, Peter
Coleman, James
Cooper, Elizabeth
Copper, Thomas
Crandell, Thomas

UNION (continued)
Dempster, Hugh
Fleming, Elizabeth
Gilpin, George
  Joseph (heirs)
  Thos. (heirs)
Hall, Jonathan (heirs)
Hepburn & Dundass
Hunter, William Jr.
  William Sr.
McClanahan, John
McCrea, Robert
McIver, John
McLiesh, James
Massett
Shreve & Lawrason
Swillers, Hawke, & Bonne

NEAR ALLEY
McCrea, Robert
Mann, Mrs.

UNION
Crandell, Thomas
Shreve & Lawrason
Slimmer, Christian

NEAR UNION
Heidie
Hughes
Reeves
Thorn, Michael

UNION
Page, William
Wales, Andrew
Watson, Josiah

WASHINGTON
Brocket, Robert
Caverly, Joseph
Heineman, Jacob
Smith, John

35

WATER
Ashton, Rich W.
Borer, John
Conway, Richard
Groods, Sam'l
Thompson, Edw. K.
Thornton, Joseph

NEAR WATER
Ellis (heirs)
Hill, George

WATER
Blunt, Washer
Brown
Clarke, Richard
Fleming, Eliz.
Gilpin, Joseph (heirs)
　　Thos. (heirs)
Hall, Jonathan (heirs)
Harrison, Robert H.
　　(estate)
Herbert, William
Hodgson, William
Hunter, William
Jenkins, Richard
Keith, James
Kirkpatrick, Thos.
　　(estate)
Mann, Bernhard
Marsteller, Philip
Pepper, Michael
Ramsay, Dennis
Roberdeau, Daniel
Shugarts, Zachariah
Slimmer, Christian
Sullivan, John
Talbot, Levi
Winterbury, John
Wools, William

NEAR WATER
Wales, Andrew

WATER
Murray, John
Shortley, Luke
Smith, Alex
Wales, Andrew
Watson, Josiah
Weston, Lewis

WHARF
Adam, Robert (estate)
Conway, Richard
Crandell, Thos.
Hodgson, William
Hooe, Robert T.
Hooe & Harrison
Spicott, Catherine
Wm. Lowrey & Co.
Wilson, William

WHARF, NEAR ADAM'S
Evans, Robert
Foushee, John

WHARF, HOOE'S
Ferguson, Cumberland
Hartshorne, William
Hartshorne & Donaldson

WHARF, KIRK'S
Hartshorne, William
Hartshorne & Donaldson

WILKES
Arell, David
Cox, Jacob
Fletcher, James
Hunter, William Jr.
　　William Sr.
Lee, Ludwell
Lutz, Michael
Peyton, Mrs.

NEAR WILKES
Nichols, Eli
Rowe, Absolom

WILKES
Faucet
Greenway, Joseph
Slacum, Gabriel
Slacum, George
Williams, Selbourn
Wright, William

WOLF
Butcher, John
Caverly, Joseph
Goodes, George

WOLF
Fitzgerald, John

NEAR WOLF
Harper, Sam'l

WOLF
Fitzgerald, John
Henly, David
Janney, Joseph
Kirk, Bridget
McWhir, William
Spooner, Nathaniel
Washington, Bushrod

OCCUPATIONS

Material taken from:
Alexandria, 1st May 1797 -

A census of the third ward with the Deficenes (sic) of the fire buckets required by Act of the Corporation Also such Nausances (sic) as we the wardens think ought to be removed you will find stated as followes in the following pages
Mungo Dykes
Ephraim Evans

4th Ward Census 1794-1795
William Bushby and George Coryele

Census Third Ward
1796
Aaron Hewes and John Korn

ATTORNEYS -
Simms, Charles

BAKERS -
Crandell, Thomas
Korn, John
Stieber, Michael
Thornton, Joseph

BANK OFFICERS -
McKenna, James

BLACKSMITHS -
Chatham, James
Faucet, John
Runtzel, Andrew
Yost, John

BLOCKMAKERS -
Blunt, Washer

BOARDING HOUSES -
Ferguson, Cumberland

BREWERS -
Balfour, James
Wales, Andrew

BRICKLAYERS -
Cook, Lewis
Hale, George
Reeves, Leonard
Rigg, John
Sullivan, John
Wright, William

CABINET MAKERS -
Steuart, John

CARPENTERS -
Dykes, Mungo
Fulmore, Joseph
Fulton, Robert
Harper, William
Shortley, Luke
Shuck, Jacob
Tatsapaw, Adam
Tatsapaw, Peter
Wilson, William
Worrell, Morris

CASHIER -
Chapin, Gurden

CHANDLER -
Resler, Jacob

CITY OFFICIALS -
Alderman
Hunter, William Jr.
Murray, John
Ramsay, Dennis
Taylor, Jesse

Common Council Member
Hannah, Nicholas
Patton, William
Porter, Thomas
Shreve, Benjamin
Wise, Peter

Mayor
Marsteller, Philip

Recorder
Winsor, Olney, Esq.

CLERK -
Deneale, George

COMBMAKER -
Duffy, John

COOPER -
Bird, William
Boyer, John
Hale, George
Hill, George

DOCTOR -
Craik, James
Dick, Elisha C.

DRAYMAN -
McCue, Henry
Mann, Bernhard

HATTER -
Hewes, Aaron

HOUSEKEEPER -
Slimmer, Christian

INSPECTOR -
Smith, Alex

JOINER -
Coryele, George

LABORERS -
Gray, Hannah or Anna

MARINERS -
Campbell, James
Copper, Thomas
Farrel, Capt. William
Slacum, George
   (shipmaster)
Spooner, Nathaniel

MERCHANTS -
Butcher, John
Coryell, George

MERCHANTS (continued)
Davy, David
Gilpin, George
Gordon, Alexander
Hampson, Bryan
Harper, Samuel
Hickman, William
Hodgson, William
Hooe, Robert T.
Irvine, Thomas
Janney, Joseph
Lawrason, James
McPherson, Isaac
Marsteller, Philip
Newton, William
Paton, William
Rogerson and Dabney
Shreve, Benjamin
Smith, Alex
Swope, Adam L.
Taylor, George
Taylor, Jesse
Thompson, Jonah
Vowell, Thomas
Watson, Josiah
Williams, Thomas
Wilson, James

MILITARY OFFICERS -
U.S. Army
Hannah, Nicholas, Capt.

Naval Officer
Reynolds, John
Fitzgerald, John

MILLSTONE MAKER -
Halley, William

NOTARY PUBLIC -
Moore, Cleon

ORDINARY KEEPER -
Rutter, George
Redman, Thomas

PAINTERS -
Bushby, William

PILOTS -
Foushee, John

PLAISTERERS -
Fletcher, James

PRINTERS -
Langston, Benj.

SADLERS -
Hayes, Andrew
Marks, William
Uhler, Valentine
Wise, John

SCHOOLMASTERS -
Edmunds, Edmond
Roberdeau, Daniel
Walker, Henry

SEAMSTRESS -
Marr, Peggy

SHIPBUILDERS -
Goodes, George
Goods, Sam
Hunter, John
Rowe, Absolom

SHIPMASTER -
Davis, Samuel

SHOEMAKERS -
Simmonds, Samuel
Winterbury, John

SHOPKEEPERS -
  Conn, Philip
  Earp, Caleb
  Evans, Robert
  Fitzpatrick, Thomas
  Maservey, Thomas
  Rutter, George
  Thornton, Joseph

SILVERSMITHS -
  Miller, Mordecai
  Sanford, Edward

STONECUTTER -
  Cook, Lewis
  Wright, William

TANNER -
  Lutz, Michael

TAYLORS -
  Harper, John
  Longdon, John
  Swillers, Joseph
  Weightman, Richard

TABACCONIST -
  Cox, Jacob (Gentleman)
  Pile, Peter

WATCHMAKER -
  Miller, Mordecai

www.ingramcontent.com/pod-product-compliance
Lightning Source LLC
Chambersburg PA
CBHW060428090426
42734CB00011B/2497